S0-ABQ-417

THE HOT Games

A Guide to the New Video Games

by
Randi Hacker

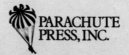

PARACHUTE PRESS, INC.

Special thanks to Charles Ardai, Bill Kunkel,
Andy Eddy, John Sauer, Matty Stine, Noah Keating,
Alex Abajian, and Hilary Wolf.

Parachute Press, Inc.
156 Fifth Avenue
New York, NY 10010

Copyright © 1989 Parachute Press, Inc.
ISBN: 0-938753-24-X

All rights reserved, which includes the right to reproduce this book in any
form whatsoever except as provided by U.S. Copyright Law. For information
address Parachute Press.

First printing: September 1989
Printed in the USA

Design by Greg Wozney

U-Force, Legacy of the Wizard, and The Battle of Olympus are registered trademarks of Broderbund
Software, Inc. Wireless-Infrared Remote Controller is a trademark of Acclaim Entertainment, Inc.
The Guardian Legend, Deadly Towers, and R-Type are trademarks of IREM Corp. Zoomer and
Ultimate™ Superstick are trademarks of Beeshu, Inc. Nintendo®, The Legend of Zelda, Metroid,
Mike Tyson's Punch Out, Mario Bros., Super Mario Bros., Super Mario Bros. 2, Zelda II™: The
Adventure of Link, Anticipation, Ice Hockey, RC Pro-Am, NES Max, Excitebike, Zapper® gun,
Hogan's Alley, Game Boy, The Power Pad, World Class Track Meet, Kid Icarus, Nintendo
Entertainment System, and Rad Racer are registered trademarks of Nintendo of America, Inc. Double
Dragon is a registered trademark of Technos Japan Corp. 1942 and Ghosts and Goblins are registered
trademarks of Capcom U.S.A. Castlevania, Blades of Steel, and Gradius are registered trademarks of
Konami Industry Co., Ltd. Top Gun logo is a trademark of Paramount Pictures Corp. Konami, Inc.
Authorized User. Spy vs. Spy is licensed from First Star Software, Inc. Sega is a registered trademark
of Sega of America, Inc. Lord of the Sword, Reggie Jackson Baseball, Altered Beast, Time Soldiers,
Genesis, Kenseiden, Miracle Warriors, The Sega Light Phaser, Shinobi, Phantasy Star, Thunder
Blade, Shanghai, Golvellius™ Valley of Doom, Poseidon Wars 3-D, Out Run, Out Run 3-D, Alex
Kidd—The Lost Stars, After Burner, Zaxxon™ 3-D, Shooting Gallery, and Space Harrier are
trademarks of Sega of America, Inc. TurboGrafx™-16 and Keigh Courage in Alpha Zones are
trademarks of NEC Home Electronics, Inc. Othello is a registered trademark licensed by Anjar Co.
California Games and The Omnicron Conspiracy are trademarks of Epyx Software, Inc. ALF is a
licensed trademark of Alien Productions. MicroLeague WWF Wrestling is a registered trademark of
MLSA. Borrowed Time is a registered trademark of Mediagenic, Inc. Star Trek: First Contact is a
registered trademark of Simon & Schuster Electronic Publishing, Inc. Superman: Man of Steel and
Beverly Hills Cop are registered trademarks of TyneSoft. Arkanoid and Rastan are registered
trademarks of Taito America Corp. Jaws is a registered trademark of LJN Industries. Bad Street
Brawler is a trademark of Beam Software. Atari® and Atari 2600® Home Video Game System™ are
registered trademarks of Atari Corporation. Pong, Space Invaders, Donkey Kong, Joust, Odyssey,
Combat, Pole Position, and Beauty and the Beast are trademarks of Atari Corporation. Freedom Stick is
a registered trademark of Camerica, Inc. ColecoVision is a trademark of Coleco, Inc. Intellivision is a
trademark of INTV, Inc. Pac Man is a registered trademark of NAMCO, Ltd. Buffalo Bill's Wild West
Show and Rodeo and Ringling Brothers' Circus Games are registered trademarks of Keypunch, Inc.
International Team Sports is a registered trademark of SportTime, Inc. Karate Kid is a registered
trademark of LJN Toys, Inc. Power Glove, Glove Pilot, Super Glove Ball, and The Terror of "Tech
Town" are registered trademarks of Mattel, Inc.

TABLE OF CONTENTS

CHAPTER ONE
Hotter Than Ever

If you want to know how to beat your friends in your favorite hot video games, read on. With THE HOT GAMES as your guide, you'll be able to increase your scores overnight! THE HOT GAMES is filled with secrets and hints and inside information on the hottest video games out there today. And it's no secret that the two hottest game systems are Nintendo® and Sega®

Today's hottest games are faster, brighter, tougher, cooler, and more powerful than ever. You can play for hours, going through dozens of screens, and never find all the secrets hidden in the program. Were video games always this complex? Of course not.

It all started with *Pong*™

Pong was the first popular arcade game. It was invented by Nolan Bushnell, the father of Atari® in 1971. The game was a simple version of Ping-Pong. A dotted line in the center of the screen was the net. Two short lines glowing at either side of the screen were the paddles. A small square of light that bounced back and forth over the net was the ball. Your job was to operate one of the paddles and hit the "ball" to your opponent—either another player or the computer. When one of you missed, the other got a point. That's all there was to it.

Compared to today's action-intensive games, *Pong* probably sounds like Dullsville. But people loved it! It became a very popular arcade game, and soon it was followed by others. There was *Space Invaders*™ in which an army of crazy-looking aliens marched down from the top of the screen. You controlled a tanklike shape that moved back and forth behind a wall at the bottom of the screen. The aliens shot at you, and you shot back at them. Another popular game was *Combat*™ in which you moved a tank through a maze and shot at another tank that was shooting at you. Simple but fun.

Then everyone went wild over *Pac-Man*.® You know the game. You were a yellow dot with a big appetite. You'd nibble your way through a maze filled with dots. Ghosts with names like Inky, Binky, and Clyde would try to catch you. If they did, you were a goner. If you ate all the dots first, you moved on to the next level, which was a lot like the first level, only harder.

As arcade games grew in popularity, their hardware and software became more advanced. First the graphics improved. Instead of lines and squares, you got little people, cars with wheels that turned, and background scenes. The sound effects became more various and theme music was added. Then the games began to tell stories. *Donkey Kong*™ was one of the first games that told a story. You were a guy named Mario who had to save his girlfriend from the clutches of a gorilla—much more complex than shoot and run!

But what about home video games? Well, by 1983 there were three main home game systems. The first was the Atari 2600® Home Video Game System.™ Then there was Intellivision.™ Finally there was ColecoVision.™ Although the home game systems were simple compared to the arcade games, people loved the idea that they could play at home whenever they wanted. And they did more than just play games. They bought video game magazines, books, and T-shirts, and held nationwide competitions. There were TV stories based on video games. Video game fever was everywhere.

Hundreds of companies made hundreds of cartridges for the home systems. Some were arcade adaptations of games like *Joust,*™ *Pac-Man,*® and *Pole Position*.™ Others were original stories made just for home game systems. There were climbing games like *Beauty and the Beast*™ in which you had to save a girl from a giant gorilla who was holding her captive at the top of a skyscraper.

But home video games were still primitive. The graphics were square and blocky, the sounds were just beeps, and the same screens kept on repeating. By the end of 1984, people got bored with them — companies stopped making them. Hardly anybody talked about them or played them anymore. It looked like the end of the video game story.

About five years passed and then, from Japan, came a new generation of home video games, including the Nintendo Entertainment System®. And Nintendo® was soon followed by Sega®! Today these game systems are still the hottest ones around. They have graphics as good as those in arcade games! They have enough memory to program in screen after screen of adventure and action! And they have incredible animation, great action, and plenty of great games that take you where no video game player has been before!

Today's games have topnotch graphics. In Nintendo's game *Blades of Steel*™, your hockey players look like real hockey players. In Sega's *Out Run*,™ you can see your character's hair blowing in the wind. And in space simulation games, if you're the pilot of a spaceship, you feel as if you're riding in the cockpit of the space shuttle Discovery.

Some of today's home games are even better than arcade games. Take *Super Mario Brothers*®, for instance. It's much more complex and exciting than Nintendo's original arcade game, *Mario Brothers*® Some home adventure games could never be played as arcade games. They look as good as arcade games and are as much fun, but they take *days* to finish! A good example of this is Nintendo's *The Legend of Zelda*,® which has 9 levels.

Will today's video game craze die out like the first one? It's not likely! Today's games are so much better than the first games. The awesome power, excellent graphics, and incredible music of today's games will probably keep kids playing video games well beyond the year 2000.

Today there are more games and systems available than ever before. Dozens of companies are making hundreds of games for several different systems. If this book were to tell you about all of them, it would have to be thousands of pages long!

That's why THE HOT GAMES focuses *only* on what's HOT. And there's no question about it—the two hottest systems around are Nintendo and Sega! In fact, over 20 million homes have either Nintendo or Sega systems. So if you want to get the inside scoop on the hottest new games, equipment, tips, and secrets for the Nintendo and Sega systems, just read on.

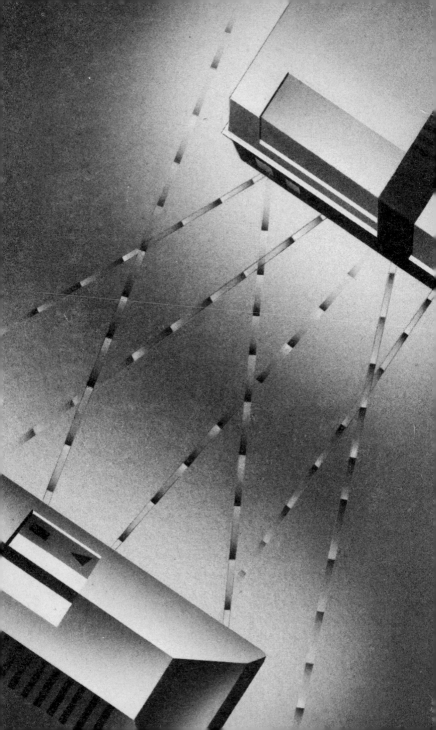

CHAPTER TWO
Battle of the Top Two

Kids everywhere are catching video game fever. Some play on Nintendo systems. Some play on Sega systems. And they're always arguing about which is better.

Which is the best system? That depends on which features are important to you. Do you want lots of games? Do you want super simulations? Or do you like the "Pause" button to be on the controller?

Here's a comparison of the Nintendo and Sega systems. Read about how they stack up against each other. Then decide for yourself which system is better for you.

GAME CONSOLES

You might say the console is the power center of any video game. Everything connects to it: the game cartridge, the control pads, and even your television set! The electronic and computer circuitry inside the console turns all these elements into a complete home entertainment system. How do the consoles of the Nintendo and Sega systems compare to each other?

Nintendo

The Nintendo game console is gray and black and a little bigger than a loose-leaf notebook. The cartridge slot is in front under a hinged door. There are two joystick ports in front. The "Power" and "Reset" buttons are built into the console.

Sega

The Sega console is black and red and a little bit smaller than a telephone book. The cartridge slot is on top at the back. There are two joystick ports and a slot for the 3-D glasses in front. The "Reset" and "Pause" buttons are on the console. This means that every time you want to stop *Double Dragon*™ in mid-kick, you've got to move your whole body to do it.

BONUS SEGA TIP: The "Pause" button can also help you access subscreens!

CONTROL PADS

The control pads are almost as important as the game cartridges. They plug into the console and let you tell your on-screen character where to move, what to pick up, and who to destroy.

Most video game systems come with two control pads. Most control pads have a direction controller and two action buttons built in. The direction controller controls

14

which way your character moves—up, down, left, or right. The action buttons control jumping and weapon use.

Which control pads would be best for your needs? Read on and find out.

Nintendo

The Nintendo control pad has a cross-shaped direction controller on the left, the "Select" and "Start" buttons in the middle, and the "A" and "B" buttons on the right. Not surprisingly, the "Start" button starts the game. You use the "Select" button to choose the difficulty level, the number of players, and your characters. The "Select" button can be used to program in code numbers that allow you to skip certain screens in a game. The "Select" button also controls the "Pause" features.

The "A" button controls the jumping, and the "B" button controls the action. For instance, by using the "B" button in *Super Mario Brothers 2*,™ you can make Mario pull up grass and throw it at his enemies. The "B" button also controls Turbo Charge, which lets you move superfast.

Pushing the controllers in special combinations can help you play a more skillful game. For example, by pressing "Up" on the direction controller while sliding your right thumb quickly from "A" to "B," you can make your character jump and use his weapons higher in the air.

BONUS NINTENDO TIP: Press down on the "Select" button at the beginning of *Mike Tyson's Punch Out*® and program in the number 007 373 5963. That will catapult you right into a match with Mike himself.

Sega

The Sega control pad is a lot like the Nintendo control pad. The direction control is on the left. The action buttons are on the right.

The two control pads have a few differences, too. The Sega direction controllers are round instead of shaped like a plus-sign. This allows you more precise control over your character's moves. With a plus-shaped direction controller you have a choice of only four directions: up, down, left, and right. With a round direction controller, you can press down on any spot on the edge of the circle and move in a combination of directions: up and left, down and right, up and right, or down and left. This gives you more control over your character.

Instead of being called "A" and "B," the buttons that control jumping and Turbo Charge on the Sega control pad are called "1" and "2." As with Nintendo, pressing "Up" on the direction controller while rapidly pressing "1" and "2" can help you jump and fight higher. The "1" button doubles as the "Start" button.

The Sega system is great for players who like to experiment! Sega's designers have programmed little surprises into their system. You can find them by pressing different combinations of the buttons on the control pad. The manufacturers call these surprises "Easter Eggs" because they're hidden.

BONUS SEGA EASTER EGG TIP: Play around with the buttons. Press them in the right combination and in certain games you'll become invincible.

SOUND

Give each system the Closed-Eye Test. Close your eyes and listen to two cartridges in each system. How do Nintendo and Sega rate in the music department?

Nintendo

Anyone who's ever played Nintendo knows that its sound is pretty terrific. No two games sound alike and the music goes very well with the type of game you're playing. *Othello*® has dramatic music. *Ghosts and Goblins*™ has a spooky soundtrack. And Nintendo music plays continuously throughout every game.

Sega

Sega is known for its high-quality sounds. Each game has its own distinctive song. You would never confuse the music from *After Burner*™ with that from *Shooting Gallery*™. The background music plays throughout each game and each level has a different tune.

BONUS SEGA SOUND EASTER EGG TIP: By pressing the right combination of buttons on the control pad, you can listen to the music from all levels of the game you're playing.

GRAPHICS AND ANIMATION

Which games look the best?

Nintendo

There's no question that Nintendo's graphics are outstanding. The colors are clear. The characters move quickly and smoothly. The background art is realistic.

Nintendo's graphics are more like cartoons than video games, and they're very close to arcade quality.

Sega

Sega's graphics are about as close as you can get to arcade quality without spending a quarter to play. The colors are bright. You can practically see the expressions on the characters' faces. The animation is almost lifelike. The background art is realistic and clear.

3-D CAPABILITY

Both Sega and Nintendo offer 3-D glasses for 3-D games. Are both 3-D systems A-1?

Before answering that question, here's a short explanation on how your own 3-D system works. You see in 3-D because you have two eyes. Each eye sees an object from a slightly different vantage point. When the two images reach your brain, it combines them and comes up with a three-dimensional picture. Instead of appearing flat, things look like they have volume and that they occupy space.

Nintendo

Nintendo's 3-D games work in the same way that 3-D comic books work. This means that the image will look blurry unless you are wearing special glasses with red and blue lenses. The graphics consist of red lines and blue lines, drawn very close together. When you look through the glasses, the red and blue lenses bring the lines together. This gives you a feeling of depth. It isn't good to play a 3-D game for long, though. You can get a headache. There aren't many 3-D games available for Nintendo now, but more are planned for the future.

Sega

Sega's 3-D games don't use a system of red and blue lines and lenses. Their glasses are electronic. They plug into the console and work on a high-speed shutter system. Special 3-D software engages the glasses and causes the shutters in each lens to open and close alternately at superspeed.

The Sega 3-D games are incredibly realistic, and there are more of them than there are for Nintendo. When you're flying down the mazelike corridors of *Zaxxon™ 3-D*, you really feel like you're moving inside three walls. And when an enemy ship bursts into flames, you almost feel as if you should run away from it! Sega has a lot of 3-D games already and will be coming out with more.

GAMES

Which company has the most games?

Nintendo

When it comes to the number of game cartridges, Nintendo wins hands-down. There are more games—over one hundred—for Nintendo than for any other system! That's because Nintendo isn't the only company making games for their system. Many other companies are licensed by Nintendo to make games for their system. And the number of categories is mind-boggling! Their selection of categories includes sports, maze, action/adventure, role playing, and arcade adaptations.

Sega

Sega's software library is much smaller than Nintendo's. But Sega has the best selection of simulations, such as *After Burner,* games with different and unusual plots, such as *Space Harrier™,* and arcade adaptations, such as *Thunder Blade™.* Sega's games also tend to be more sophisticated than Nintendo's.

TARGET GAMES

Both Nintendo and Sega have guns for use with target-shooting games. The Nintendo Zapper® gun and the Sega

Light Phaser™ operate in basically the same way when it comes to aiming and shooting.

Sega's target-shooting games have a feature that Nintendo's does not. They have a backdrop that gives important visual feedback. For example, if your shot misses the target, it doesn't just disappear into space as it does in a Nintendo game. It rips into the backdrop and leaves a hole. This lets you see your mistake and correct it on your next shot.

CHAPTER THREE
Game Strategies

Tips, hints, and secrets to help you win!

NINTENDO

Super Mario Brothers 2™

The Story: Mario has come a long way since his first star-ring role in *Donkey Kong*. From *Super Mario Brothers 1* to *Super Mario Brothers 2*, the Mario brothers are back in another adventure. You're either Mario, Luigi, the Princess, or Toad. Wart, the Big Boss, has put the Land of Dreams under his spell and has created the monsters Cobrat, Ninji, and the three-headed Tryclyde by playing with the Dream Machine. To save the Land of Dreams, you have to find Wart and hit him with giant mushrooms and radishes. Wart just hates vegetables!

HINTS, TIPS, AND SECRETS

● Before you leave one world to go to the next, be sure you have full strength. You'll be dressed in white if you do.

● Never leave a screen until you've collected everything you can find. You can't always go back to pick up something you missed.

● Floating Brick Walls are *more* than just floating brick walls. There are treasures hidden inside them: coins, magic potions, flowers that make you grow, and more. The first time you go through any level, jump and hit *all* the floating bricks with your head. Keep jumping and butting them with your head. When the brick lines disappear, you know you've absorbed all the power that's inside.

● Anything you can stand on, you can pick up. Anything you pick up, you can throw. Anything you can throw can be useful against some enemy. In an emergency, you can even jump on top of one of your enemies, and then pick him up and throw him at another enemy.

● At the end of level 1-1, run toward the flagpole while you press "A" and "B" and "Forward." If you leap high enough, you can get from 800 to 5,000 points.

● In level 4-2, use coins to make steps if you need to.

● There are vases at the end of each board on levels 1-3, 4-2, and 5-3. If you go down them, you can warp ahead to levels 4, 6, and 7.

Mike Tyson's Punch Out:

The Story: You're an up-and-coming young boxer. You want to fight the champ for the title of Heavyweight Champion of the World. But first you have to punch your way up through the ranks.

HINTS, TIPS, AND SECRETS

● In your first few bouts, alternate jabs and body blows without stopping. Don't even bother to duck or block. If you come out swinging, you can knock your opponent down before he can even touch you.

● Green Tiger is a magic fighter, but that doesn't mean you can't beat him. When he hits you with his magic punch, he gets dizzy. Take advantage of his dizziness and hit him!

● Don't try to outpunch Mike Tyson or you'll be flat on your back before you know it. The secret to beating Mike Tyson is a good defense. Keep your hands up and block all his attacks. Meanwhile, watch for an opening. Then go for it!

● For more energy, press "Start" and "Select" constantly.

The Legend of Zelda
The Story: You're an elf named Link. Your job is to save the land of Hyrule. To do this, you have to hunt all over Hyrule for the eight pieces of the TriForce of Power, fight the evil overlord, Ganon, and free the imprisoned Princess Zelda.

HINTS, TIPS, AND SECRETS

● Whenever you see a few stone blocks in a room, push on them. Stairs or doors are sometimes hidden underneath.

● Listen to what the people in the cave have to say. One of them will give you the secret for defeating Ganon.

● The magic power of the whistle is great. It's *the* secret weapon to use against the big-eared, noise-hating Pols Voice. It will also open some of the game's magic passages.

● Don't use Link's special weapons on ordinary creatures. Whenever you can, use your sword. Save magic for the most powerful monsters.

Zelda II™: The Adventure of Link™

The Story: Link has grown since his first adventure. Now he's 16 and Hyrule has gotten itself into a new mess. Even though Ganon is dead, his henchmen are terrorizing the kingdom. Another princess named Zelda needs to be rescued and, somehow, the TriForce has been scattered again. As Link, you have to collect the TriForce, break the spell on Zelda, and stop Ganon's henchmen from using *your* blood to bring Ganon back to life.

HINTS, TIPS, AND SECRETS

- There are separate fight scenes. Practice by fighting the weak enemies first.
- Know what the monsters look like. The weakest ones are those shaped like circles with eyes.
- Know a monster's weak spots *before* you get into a fight with it. For instance, you can only kill the Geldarm by hitting it on the head.
- Pick up all the Magic Containers. You can't learn powerful magic without them.
- When you find a town, look for swordsmen and magicians. They'll give you the new skills you'll need to defeat the strongest monsters in the King's Palace.
- Don't go spell crazy. Spells use up precious magic points, and they're usually only good for one screen. Only use spells when you absolutely must.
- Don't let the Octarods get you!

Metroid®

The Story: A strange and deadly life-form was found floating deep in space. Before it could be destroyed, pirates stole it. Now they're using it to control the galaxy. The Federation Police have sent you to the pirates' planet-fortress on a find-and-destroy mission.

HINTS, TIPS, AND SECRETS

● The most important power tools are the Varia and the Ice Beam. The Varia saves your energy when you're attacked. The Ice Beam is the weapon you must use in the final battle against the Metroid.

● The final battle against the Metroid is *not* the last fight in the game! You *still* have to fight the Mother Brain and the Zeebetite coils that feed her energy. After that, there's one more secret battle to fight. So, be sure to save some strength and weapons to finish the game.

Rad Racer™

The Story: You're a driver in a cross-country race. You can drive either one of two super cars: a 328 Twin Turbo or an F1 Machine. You're racing against Lamborghinis and Porsches, so you have to floor it as often as possible without wiping out. *Rad Racer* also has a 3-D mode. Special 3-D glasses are included in the game.

HINTS, TIPS, AND SECRETS

● No matter how nice the scenery is, keep your eyes on the road! This is especially important in Stage 7, where weather is bad and the curves can be tricky.

● Unless there's no other way to avoid an accident, don't use the brakes at all. And unless you're sure you can stay on the road, don't use the Turbo Charge. You won't gain as much time with Turbo Charge as you'll lose if you crash.

● Use the 3-D glasses for a short time only. They can make it hard to judge the distance between cars. They'll also make your eyes tired. If you want to play the game straight to the end, use the standard mode.

Castlevania™

The Story: You're a young lad, and you are sent to save a

princess from the evil Dracula. As you search through his spooky castle you have to battle flying Medusas, vampire bats, zombies, and black leopards. There's also a horrible crushing machine to get through and the sinister Queen Medusa to defeat. Your weapons include boomerangs, swords, whips, and a morning star.

HINTS, TIPS, AND SECRETS

- Whip everything—even the walls! There are treasures hidden behind the stones.
- The candles mounted high on the castle walls have treasures in them. To whip them, press "Up," then "A" "B." That will give you extra height in your jump.
- Don't worry about Frankenstein. He's harmless.
- Timing is everything. Don't try to run straight through the crushing machine. Stop and rest by the stone pillars between each crusher.

Anticipation™

The Story: This is Nintendo's first computer board game. You move your pieces around an on-screen board and try to identify the pictures the computer draws. There are sixteen categories such as "Food," "Weaponry," and "Music." There are four skill levels and surprises hidden all over. You can play against the computer or with up to three friends.

HINTS, TIPS, AND SECRETS

- Keep the category in mind as the Video Pencil draws its picture. If the category is "Clothing," the answer won't be "fish" or "motorboat," no matter what you think the picture looks like.
- Buzz in as soon as you think you know the answer. You'll still get a few seconds to think about the puzzle, but the other players won't be able to buzz in and answer before you.

- To practice, try playing a four-player game by yourself. Since you won't be racing against other players or the computer, you'll be able to test yourself with lots of puzzles.

International Team Sports™
The Story: You're a camper competing in ten activities, such as tug of war, skateboard racing, six-legged racing, crab walking, and belly bump ball. This is one of Nintendo's Power Pad™ games. You and the other players run in place on a special floor mat to control the action.

HINTS, TIPS, AND SECRETS
- For the jumping events—Log Hop, Water Cross, and Wall Jump—you can get ahead by jumping entirely off the pad and onto the floor. Then get back on the pad. The pad will think you stayed up in the air all the time you were off it!
- You can pump your bubble faster in the Bubble Race if you use your feet instead of your hands.

Ice Hockey™
The Story: This game follows the rules of real ice hockey. Each team tries to hit the puck into the other team's goal. If the score is tied after three periods, the game is decided by penalty shots.

HINTS, TIPS, AND SECRETS
- Each team has four players. Each player has different weaknesses and strengths. When you make up your team, try to choose a balance of players. Take some who are fast but weak and some who are strong but slow.
- When you want to shoot the puck, press "B" and hold it down. If you press and release it quickly, you'll make a "Fake Shot" and might lose a chance to score.
- If you want to start a fight, go up to the player with the

puck and press "A."

● Remember, a player can be penalized and kept out of the game. If one of your teammates is serving a penalty, don't start a fight. Your team is already short a player, and you risk being penalized yourself. You don't want to rack up too many penalties or your team will lose the game.

Kid Icarus™
The Story: The monster Medusa has captured the goddess Palutena and has Angel Land in her power. Using your angel wings, your bow and arrow, and other weapons you pick up, you have to destroy Medusa, save Palutena, and make the world safe for angels everywhere.

HINTS, TIPS, AND SECRETS
● Buying from the Black Market is the *only* way to get your treasures back if they are stolen by Pluton or Pluton-Fly.

● If you don't have enough money to buy something on the Black Market, use your credit card. But remember you won't be able to charge anything on it again until you've paid off your debt.

● Make your own map. That way you won't have to spend money on Pencils, the on-screen map-making service.

● If you've broken all but one pitcher in the treasure chambers, don't touch the last one. It contains the God of Poverty, who will steal all your treasures.

● If you see the Eggplant Wizard, run! His spells won't kill you but they can turn you into an eggplant. Then you'll have to waste a lot of time getting the spell reversed. And wasting time will delay you from reaching Palutena and finishing the game.

SEGA

Double Dragon

The Story: You are either Billy (aka Hammer) or Jimmy Lee (aka Spike) — two tough dudes. One of your enemies has kidnapped your girlfriend, and you've got to save her by fighting every gang you meet. You can use your hands, feet, and other weapons you pick up along the way.

HINTS, TIPS, AND SECRETS

• Your elbow jab is your strongest attack. Use it against the gang lords. Remember, you've got to be facing away from your enemy to do it.

• There's a secret on level 4. When your character appears, jump up and down about thirty times. You'll be invincible for the rest of the level!

Phantasy Star™

The Story: You must travel to the Algol star system to overthrow the evil tyrant Lassic. Along the way you visit three planets, fight alien creatures in dungeons, and find out just how tough crossing a desert can be.

HINTS, TIPS, AND SECRETS

• You can get some money right away — just look in the cave in the upper right-hand corner.

• After you talk to the leader in the Eppi Forest, go back to the cave where you first found the money. You'll find the key that opens the locked dungeons.

• When you're crossing the lava pit, don't stop to fight. If you do, you'll get fried! If you're lucky enough to have the Hovercraft, use it to get across.

• You need the Mirrorshield to fight Medusa. Here's how to get it: On the planet of Montavia, there's a gas city called Sopia. Go into it, find the mayor, and give him

31

$400. Then leave town and walk to the water. You'll see an island. Take the Hovercraft you find to the island. Get out and walk until you see an Ant Lion standing on a cactus. Stand on the cactus, too. Then choose "Search" from the menu, and the Mirrorshield will be yours.

● Before you fight Lassic, build up your strength. Here's how: After you fall through three pit traps, you'll find yourself in a hall. From there, go right, make two turns, take three steps, and face left. A secret door will appear. Go through it, down the corridor, and through a magic door. You'll find a batch of hamburgers. Gobble them up, and then go fight Lassic!

Miracle Warriors™

The Story: You are a knight and must save the Five Lands from the Dark Lord, Terrarin. To do this you must climb mountains, sail the sea, slay monsters, and behave in a knightly way.

HINTS, TIPS, AND SECRETS

● Don't get confused. Some things in the game have two names. Turo is the same person as Treo. The Shield of Ulysses is the same as the Odysseus Shield. And Iason's Monument and Gorkis Shrine are the same, too.

● Get as many magic weapons as you can before entering Iason's Monument (Gorkis Shrine). You might find some things inside the monument but it's better to prepare beforehand.

● You need three keys. You'll find them sixteen squares to the west, sixteen squares to the south, and ten squares to the north of Tegea. Use the "Come, Iason" spell to make the keys appear.

Shanghai™

The Story: This is a 3,000-year-old Chinese strategy game. There's a big stack of tiles. Each tile has a picture

on it. If you can find two tiles that match and that don't
have other tiles on top of them, you can remove them.
The object is to remove all the tiles before time runs out.

HINTS, TIPS, AND SECRETS
● *Shanghai* is very complicated, but there's a simpler version hidden inside. Here's how to get to it: When the title
screen comes up, press "Pause" at least ten times. Then
start the game. When the menu appears, choose "Game,"
then "Start Solitaire," then "Load Stored Pattern." From
the list of Stored Patterns, choose "Secret Game."

Spy vs. Spy™
The Story: Straight from the pages of *Mad* magazine
come the adventures of the black spy and the white spy. In
this game, the spies are in a race to find some top-
secret plans and then escape by plane. You are one of the
spies. You and the enemy spy set traps for each other and
fight. One trap, for example, is arranging buckets of
water to spill on the other spy's head. One person can play
against the computer or two players can play against each
other.

HINTS, TIPS, AND SECRETS
● The first thing to do is find the bag. It lets you carry
more than one thing at a time. Since there's only one bag
in the game, it's important to find it before the other
spy does.
● Beware! You can get caught in your own traps. So
remember where you put them, and try to watch where
the other spy puts his. You don't want to get caught in
either.

Shinobi™
The Story: You're a Ninja battling against a group of evil
terrorists. You have to use Ninja magic and martial-arts
weapons to save the hostages and destroy the Ring of Fire.

HINTS, TIPS, AND SECRETS

- You can start on any level you want. Just press "Down" when the title screen appears. Then press "2." Then use the control pad to select the number of the scene you want to enter.
- The easiest way to kill the green Ninjas is to hit them twice in the feet.
- To kill flying Ninjas, hit them twice while they're in the air.

Alex Kidd — The Lost Stars™

The Story: Alex Kidd stars in many Sega games. This Alex Kidd game sends you bouncing through seven alien worlds. You have to collect stars and other special items to help Alex get past the creatures who want to stop him.

HINTS, TIPS, AND SECRETS

- When you're underwater in levels 4 and 11, use your shots sparingly. The "S" star which gives you extra shots doesn't show up as often as it does on other levels.
- Don't be afraid to take chances. This game lets you Continue as often as you like after a game ends. This means you can try wild things you might not try in games that let you Continue only three times.

Kenseiden™

The Story: Evil sorcerers have invaded ancient Japan. You have to fight them in the streets and in their castles through sixteen levels to save Japan's honor.

HINTS, TIPS, AND SECRETS

- You can start on any level. Just hold down buttons "1" and "2" *before* you turn on the system. Keep holding the buttons down as you turn on the game. Release them when the title screen appears. Press the top left section of the direction controller and button "1" at the same time.

Then select the number of the round you want by using the direction controller. To start the game, press "1" or "2."

● There are two hidden Gourds of Life in round 2. To get the first one, go to the statue of Buddha. Climb onto its shoulders and jump up. You'll land in a secret room, where you'll find the first Gourd. To find the second one, go back to the Buddha and leave the room to the left. Keep going left through about three rooms until you come to another statue of Buddha. Climb onto its shoulders and jump up. You'll find the second Gourd of Life.

● In round 4, you can get an extra life. Here's how: Climb the stairs to the topmost level. In the upper right corner, you'll find a wooden doll. Take it.

Golvellius™ Valley of Doom

The Story: Demons are holding Princess Rena captive in the Valley of Doom. You're the only one who can rescue her. You journey through 150 screens of desert, ocean, forest, swamp, and beach to reach and destroy the evil Golvellius.

HINTS, TIPS, AND SECRETS

● Golvellius can't shoot while he's moving. In the final battle, keep running around him. When he starts following you, hit him with your sword.

● When you kill monsters, blue bubbles appear. Collect them to regain lost energy.

● There are passageways hidden under rocks. In the Ocean, hit the rocks on the right side of the island to find an entrance. In the Desert, you'll find blue rocks in two diamond patterns. Hit the rocks above the bottom point of the smaller diamond, and you'll find another entrance. In the Pine Forest, hit the red rock in the upper right-hand corner. There is an entrance there, too.

R-Type™

The Story: You're a lone rebel in an R-9 spaceship fighting against the Bydo Empire. The R-9 can split in two! You use this ability plus your lasers and satellites to defeat eight levels of Bydo bad guys.

HINTS, TIPS, AND SECRETS

● You can make yourself invincible for the whole game. Here's how: Before you turn the system on, hold down the lower right-hand corner of the direction controller on control pad #1. At the same time, you hold down button "1" on control pad #2. Have a friend turn the system on for you since your two hands will be busy. Keep the two buttons depressed until the title screen appears.

● You can enter a special Sound Test mode. When the Continue screen comes on after Game Over, turn the direction controller counterclockwise until the countdown reaches "O." You can listen to all the sound effects by using the direction controller and pushing button "1."

● There's a secret level. When you get to the fourth stage, look for two blank screen areas. Move the R-9 into the one on the left, and hit the left wall with the back of the ship. The secret level will start.

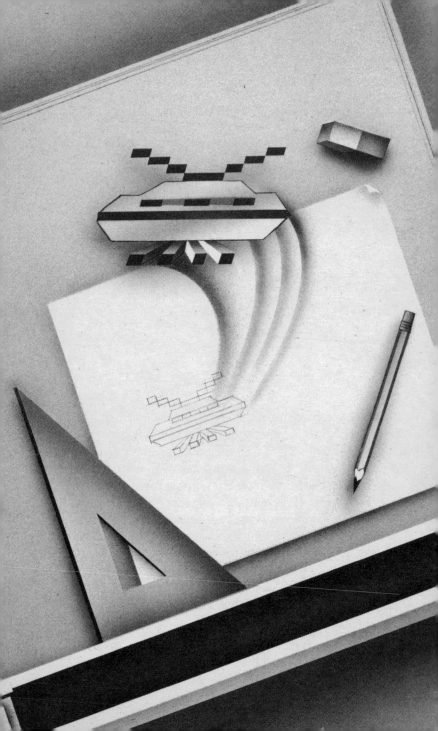

CHAPTER FOUR
Behind the Screens

While you play any of the video games described in this book, you've got a lot on your mind. You may have to keep out of danger and find the rock that hides a secret door. Or you may have to figure out how to destroy Gohma, the giant crab monster. (Aim at his eye with your bow and arrow. His eye is his weak spot.)

But once the enemy bosses are defeated and the princess is rescued, you might start wondering about the people who invent video games. Who actually *chooses* the rock that hides the secret door? What are the people like who come up with monster-destroying strategies? How do they think of ideas for different games? Do they have fun? What games do *they* like to play?

Bill Kunkel and Arnie Katz are two designers for Subway Software. They used to be the editors of *Electronic Games Magazine* — one of the first magazines about video games and computer games. Since they started Subway Software, they've created many games, including *MicroLeague WWF Wrestling*™ starring Hulk Hogan, *Borrowed Time*,™ *Star Trek: First Contact*,™ *Superman: Man of Steel*,™ *The Omnicron Conspiracy*,™ and *Beverly Hills Cop*.™ Their latest game, *Ringling Brothers' Circus Games*,™ is for Nintendo.

If anyone knows the inside story of video and computer game design, Bill and Arnie do.

~~~~~~

BONUS NINTENDO TIP: In *Karate Kid*,™ collect as many C's as you can. They give you Crane Kicks. And, unlike in school, D's are even better than C's! They give you Drum Punches!

~~~~~~

Q: What goes into designing a video game?

BILL: Well, first there's the brainstorming session. That's great. We, at Subway Software, all just sit around and think up ideas. We just let our minds go wild. We say "What if . . ." and try to come up with situations that might make fun video games.

ARNIE: But designing a game is not just coming up with a good idea. Just saying "What if there were a game where a young writer is sucked through a time warp and becomes King of England" is not enough. That part is less than 1% of the finished product.

Q: What's next?

BILL: After we decide on a story, we write the specs.

Q: Specs? What are specs?

BILL: Specs is short for "specifications." Specs for a video game are pages and pages of description. They describe everything about a game: every possible action a player can take, every object that may appear on screen, and every possible way a player can interact with the objects, characters, and other elements of the game.

Q: Do you have to write all this down?

ARNIE: Yes. A good design spec can be from 50 to 140 pages long, depending on what kind of game it is! Take *Ringling Brothers' Circus Games*, for instance. It's an action-strategy game with four events. Everything must be described! That's a lot of writing!

Q: Does writing it all down get boring?

ARNIE: No. Every design spec is different because every game is different. You find yourself doing a lot of unusual things when you design games. For example, we have a game coming out called *Buffalo Bill's Wild West Show and Rodeo*.™ In developing this game, we had to figure out how to describe what it felt like to ride a bull. We did some research but ended up having to rely on our imagination.

Q: What else goes into designing a game?

BILL: Well, we have to draw storyboards. A storyboard is a series of detailed drawings that show exactly what each screen will look like. The drawings show the position of objects in a screen and how the characters will move. The storyboard shows the programmer what action to program.

Q: You mean you don't do the programming yourself?

ARNIE: We do the design at Subway Software, but the art, music, programming, and packaging are all done elsewhere by other people. It's a team effort.

BILL: Think of us as the architects of the game. We put together the blueprint — the specs and the storyboards. Then we hand them over to a contractor — in this case a software company. The contractor hires programmers to "build" the game.

Q: Have video games always been made this way?

ARNIE: No. In the first video game boom, one designer would try to do everything. One person, usually a computer hobbyist-turned-pro, sat in front of his computer. He came up with the concept, did the graphics, programmed in "beep beep boop boop" for sound effects, and wrote the title page and the documentation. Of course, in those days there wasn't very much memory in the software to work with. You couldn't do great graphics. You couldn't do music — all you had were sound effects. You couldn't create a very complex game, so it wasn't important to have an expert design or program the play action. So one guy really *could* do everything.

These days it's quite different. Games have an incredible amount of memory. There's no way one person can excel in everything that goes into a game. So the team approach was developed. Professional designers like us design the games. A programmer programs it. A musician puts down the sound and a computer artist develops the graphics. There also might be someone who specializes in sound effects and someone who specializes in animation. It's a team effort all the way. That's how it's done in Japan, too.

Q: Tell us a little bit more about *Ringling Brothers' Circus Games*.

BILL: Sure. *Circus Games* takes circus events like tightrope walking, trapeze artistry, trick riding, and lion and tiger taming, and makes them into video games. You become a lion tamer or a trapeze artist or a tightrope walker.

ARNIE: In our specs, we had to describe how a guy with a pole in his hands would balance on a tightrope in a way that would make the player *feel* like he or she is doing the balancing act.

Q: How did you get started as designers?

BILL: Well, we had thought about it for years, even in the old days when we worked for *Electronic Games*. Then a game company called Interplay asked us to write a story for a game called *Borrowed Time*. They worked very closely with us and taught us the ins and outs of game designing.

Q: Subway Software did a game called *Beverly Hills Cop*. What's it like to adapt a video game from a movie?

ARNIE: Different. Very different. Bill, Joyce Worley (the third designer at Subway Software), and I went to see both *Beverly Hills Cop* movies with notebooks in hand. We went separately so we wouldn't influence each other. Then we all met and talked about the characters, plots, and scenery that make *Beverly Hills Cop* what it is. Then we created a game that is, in a way, a brand-new *Beverly Hills Cop* movie. The plot is new, and you're the star. You play the game and the story advances.

Q: Bill, you used to write comics. What comics did you work for?

BILL: Superman, Spiderman, Dr. Strange, Daredevil, and Richie Rich.

Q: Did that help you to design Subway Software's *Superman: Man of Steel*?

BILL: Definitely. We designed *Superman* as a sort of electronic comic book. In it you're Superman fighting a tag team of Lex Luthor and Darkseid. You get to call on all of Superman's super powers: heat vision, super breath, X-ray vision, and so on. Only you can't use two at a time.

Q: What makes a video game good?

ARNIE: Arcade quality. By that I mean a game that's colorful, exciting, action-oriented, and easy to learn but difficult to master.

BILL: Originality is important, too. When I used to go to the arcades, every time I walked to a different machine, I saw a different game. Too many games today are not original. They're just remakes of old games.

Q: What are your favorite games?

BILL: *Arkanoid*™ is fantastic. It's the kind of game I'd like to see more of. And *Double Dragon* is excellent, too. But *Jaws*™ is my favorite. *Jaws* is original and fun. Even though a lot of the elements are similar to other games—you build up power, you find treasures, you fight enemies—they're put together in a way that makes a very different and original game. And the first-person view from the ship at the end of *Jaws* is awesome.

ARNIE: *Metroid* is excellent, too. And so is *RC Pro-Am*™. It's one of the nicest of all the new Nintendo games.

Q: What's your least favorite game?

Left to right: Arnie Katz, Joyce Worley, Bill Kunkel.

BILL: Any game that uses horizontal scrolling and a side view of a running, somersaulting, shooting, or jumping character. There are far too many games like that.

Q: What makes video and computer games so great?

BILL: They open players up to experiences they couldn't have anywhere but on a computer. You can be a test pilot. You can dive underwater. You can be *inside* a pinball game. These are things you couldn't do in real life or, if you *could* do them, you'd be putting yourself at great risk. It's like living your fantasies. It's like a dream.

Q: What's your favorite part of designing?

BILL: Brainstorming. Getting together and thinking and talking and then suddenly, getting THE IDEA!

45

Q: What part do you hate the most?

BILL: Sitting down and working out the millions of details that go into every game. If I make one little change anywhere in the story, I have to go back and redo the whole structure. You have to keep good notes!

Q: What advice would you give kids who want to be game designers?

BILL: Dream. Don't be afraid to say "What if. . ." Look everywhere for your ideas. Anything can be an inspiration. Even the pattern of candy in a candy dish can be a game screen. Think of what sort of world you'd like to experience but can't, and then create it yourself. Just dream.

BONUS NINTENDO TIP: In *Gradius*™ to gain 30 extra lives, punch in this code: Up, Up, Down, Down, Left, Right, Left, Right, B, A, B, Start, Start.

CHAPTER FIVE
The Right Stuff

There are many accessories for video games and systems that can help you improve your gaming skills. Almost anything you can imagine — from a remote-control joystick to a controller you play with your feet — is available.

GOING REMOTE

Are wires and cables cramping your style? Do you wish you could walk around the room and play *The Legend of Zelda*? Here are a few remote controllers that will free you up.

The Freedom Stick™
For: Nintendo, Sega, and Atari
By: Camerica

The Freedom Stick is an infrared controller. It sends out a signal that's picked up by a receiver that plugs into the controller port on your game console. As long as the Freedom Stick is facing the receiver, you can play from anywhere in the room. Don't let anything get between the Freedom Stick and the receiver, though. It could cost you your life in a battle with the Octarods!

The Freedom Stick looks very much like the Nintendo control pad but instead of a directional cross, it has a small joystick. It also has a switch labeled "Auto/Man." When on "Auto," it makes the "A" and "B" buttons auto-repeating. This is useful when you need rapid fire or a quick series of jumps. The Freedom Stick uses four AA batteries.

BONUS NINTENDO TIP: In *Zelda II: The Adventure of Link*, go to the Eastern Continent. Then go through the cave to a small forest. You'll find a hammer in the second row of trees. Take it.

Ultimate™ Superstick
For: Nintendo and Sega
By: Beeshu

Video game players can play more quickly *and* more slowly with the wireless Ultimate Superstick. Don't be confused. The Ultimate Superstick has a Slow Motion switch that slows the game action down to give you time to think. It also has "Dial-a-Speed" buttons that let you program your auto-fire speed as high as thirty shots per second. Think of how handy that would be in a feverish battle against Kraid and Ridley, *Metroid*'s mad mini-bosses!

The Ultimate Superstick also has two sets of "Fire/Jump" buttons and a joystick direction controller.

BONUS SEGA TIP: In *Metroid*, fight Kraid and Ridley from a distance. Shoot and run. If you let them touch you more than once, you're a goner. Be especially careful of Ridley. His fire-blasts can hit you while you're running away.

The Wireless-Infrared Remote Controller™
For: Nintendo
By: Acclaim

By using the Wireless-Infrared Remote Controller, you can zap sub-bosses and battle *Castlevania*'s Queen

Medusa from as far away as thirty feet from your set!
Like the Freedom Stick, this remote controller has a
receiver that plugs into the controller port of your console.
There's even rapid-fire action for your high speed needs.
It uses four AAA batteries.

HAND, FOOT, AND FINGER CONTROLS

Take control of your score with these controls!

The Power Pad ™
For: Nintendo
By: Nintendo

Get ready to Nintendocise! That's one way of referring
to exercising and playing your Nintendo at the same time.
You can do this by using The Power Pad. The Power Pad is
a big plastic mat with red and blue circles on it. It plugs
into the control deck and lies on the floor in front of your
TV. To control the on-screen action, you step on the circles with your feet. Your character runs and jumps as fast
and as high as you do. The Power Pad comes packaged
with a *World Class Track Meet* ™ that lets you compete in track events like the high hurdles, the 100-yard
dash, and the long jump. You can play against the computer or against your friends.

There's at least one other game that you can Nintendocise with by using The Power Pad. It's called *International
Team Sports*.™ In it, you compete against the computer or
your friends in events like skateboarding, logrolling, and
tug of war.

Zoomer ™
For: Nintendo, Sega, and Atari
By: Beeshu

Here's a controller that's shaped like a steering wheel. It
has two fire buttons built into the handle, a programmable auto-fire, and a " Slow Motion" switch. When using

Zoomer, you'll find that taking the wheel in games like *Excitebike*,™ *After Burner*, and *1942*™ is really taking the wheel!

BONUS NINTENDO TIP: In *1942*, go under the wing of the huge green plane to avoid getting hit by the bullets it shoots out its back.

NES Max™
For: Nintendo
By: Nintendo
NES Max may be just what you're looking for. That is, if you don't like the direction controller on the control pad that comes with the Nintendo system. With two "Turbo

Charge" buttons and a round direction controller, NES Max lets you move anywhere on the screen at twice the usual speed! Watch out, *Rad Racers*!

BONUS NINTENDO TIP: In *Rad Racer*, don't brake before a sharp turn. Instead, stop accelerating as soon as you see the road sign. Halfway through the curve, speed up again. You lose less time this way.

READ ALL ABOUT IT

Game magazines can keep you up-to-date and informed about what's hot and what's not for your system!

Nintendo Power

Nintendo Power is the magazine put out by Nintendo for Nintendo fans. Every month it's filled with information and news about Nintendo. The magazine gives you play-by-play tips on how to beat your worst enemies, the latest news on the hottest games, top-secret techniques, posters, contests, interviews with Power Players, and top scores sent in by readers. The subscription cost is $15 a year. For more information, call 1-800-521-0900.

Team Sega Newsletter

The *Team Sega Newsletter* is filled with tips, news, and interviews with John Sauer, the man whose job is to play Sega games before anyone else does. And, in each issue, there's a high-score challenge. Here's how it works: Team Sega names the game. You play it. Then, you take a picture of your score and send it in. If it's the highest score, it will be printed in the next *Newsletter*. To receive the

Newsletter, send in the warranty card on your Sega system or just your name and address to:

Team Sega Newsletter
P.O. Box 2167
573 Forbes Boulevard
South San Francisco, CA 94080

VideoGames & Computer Entertainment Magazine

Whether you own a Nintendo, Sega, or Atari system, *VideoGames & Computer Entertainment* has news for you. *VG & CE* covers all the latest hardware, software, and super accessories for both video games and computer games. *VG & CE* also has exclusive, inside stories on all the hottest gaming equipment. To subscribe, send a check for $19.95 to:

VideoGames & Computer Entertainment Magazine
P.O. Box 16927
North Hollywood, CA 91695

BONUS NINTENDO TIP: In *Mike Tyson's Punch Out*, when you see a star above a fighter's head, press "Start." Your next punch will be a supercharged uppercut!

CHAPTER SIX
Coming Attractions

If you think what's out there is hot, wait until you see what's coming!

There's a whole world of exciting new controllers and games on their way.

CONTROL CENTRAL

Take a look at some of the new controllers.

U-Force™
For: Nintendo
By: Broderbund

It's not a joystick. It's not a control pad. It's not a steering wheel or a light gun. It's U-Force, and it's new and it's

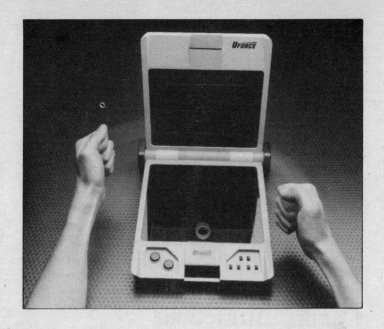

unlike anything you've ever seen. When it's folded up, U-Force looks like a small plastic briefcase. Open it and you unleash an invisible field of force that will change the way you play video games.

Instead of pressing a direction controller and slipping your thumb from "A" to "B" while pressing the "Select" button, all you have to do is move your hands within the field of force, Whatever you do inside the field will show up as a move in the game you're playing. So, if you want to throw a left hook at Mike Tyson, go ahead! Maybe you'll knock him out! Or say you're playing *Top Gun.*™ Just grab a phantom steering wheel and control your plane that way. U-Force even works with *Super Mario Brothers 2.* You use one hand to bounce and the other hand to open doors.

U-Force can be used lying flat or opened at a right angle. It plugs into the Nintendo joystick port and doesn't need batteries. Special switches on U-Force allow you to program it for play with just about every available Nintendo game. If you prefer a more hands-on control, U-Force also comes with "firing handles" and a T-bar.

Power Glove ™
For: Nintendo
By: Mattel

The Power Glove looks like something Darth Vader might wear. It's a black elbow-length glove studded with gleaming silver controls and buttons. Slip your hand into this high-tech controller, and your hand will be transformed into a finely tuned video game command module.

The Power Glove is filled with sensors that pick up every movement your hand makes right down to the twitch of your little finger. Every movement you make causes your on-screen character to do something. You can aim a lethal karate chop at an enemy in *Karate Kid*. Or use your hand to steer in *Rad Racer*. If you find you're going too fast in a driving game, just flatten your hand and push down to put on the brakes.

The Power Glove is also programmable. You can add Turbo Charge for rapid repeat action or put a game into slow motion if it's too difficult and you want to practice. The Power Glove's built-in computer keyboard even lets you customize games by choosing which fingers will control which action.

The Power Glove works with all the Nintendo games. Some new games are being developed especially for Power Glove play. Here's a preview.

Super Glove Ball ™ is a 3-D racquetball game. To play, you have to knock colored tiles off the walls and ceilings of a maze of rooms. But watch out for the mysterious creatures that pop up now and then! They'll need a good bonk on the head to keep them in line.

Glove Pilot ™ puts you in control of a spaceship and

sends you on missions to six worlds. The Power Glove lets you "reach" into the game to set the dials and switches on the spaceship's instrument panel. In *Glove Pilot*, you also get to salvage wrecked fighters, pick up air and soil samples from distant planets, and do battle using advanced weapons systems.

The Terror of "Tech Town"™ places you in a 3-D, high-tech world of the future. You search for "tech units" that you need to survive. The Power Glove acts as a robot's claw that picks up these tech units from under your enemy's nose.

Bad Street Brawler™ is a skill and action game. You use the Power Glove to perform wrestling moves and powerful karate kicks in order to defeat the evil bosses at each level.

~~~~~~

BONUS NINTENDO TIP: On level 1-2 of *Super Mario Brothers*, climb up between the wall and the left edge of the screen. Then run along the top of the screen until you get to the elevator platform. You *won't* get killed!

~~~~~~

SUPER SYSTEMS

Tomorrow's game systems will be smaller, faster, and more powerful than today's systems. Here's a sample of some of them.

TurboGrafx™-16
By: NEC

One of the most popular video game systems in Japan is finally coming to the United States. It's called the TurboGrafx -16 home entertainment system. It's small. It's light. And it's powerful.

Each TurboGrafx -16 game is no bigger than a credit card, but there is nothing small about the graphics or game play. The TurboGrafx -16 will come packed with one TurboPad controller and one adventure game called *Keith Courage™ in Alpha Zones.*™ This game is set in the year 2017, thirteen years after a giant meteor collided with Earth. All the countries of the world have banded together to form one unified nation called N.I.C.E. (Nations of International Citizens). You, as Keith Courage, lead N.I.C.E. in its fight against the Beastly Alien Dudes (B.A.D.) who have built a seven-level city beneath the Earth's surface. You have four friends to help you: Nurse Nancy, who has the power to heal your wounds;

Weapons Master, who sells swords; Wise Wizard, who gives you magic devices that will help you in battle; and the Prophet, who has good advice. You also have a special nova suit that allows you to assume the powers of a super robot.

These other peripherals will be sold separately to add to the excitement of the TurboGrafx-16 system:

● The TurboGrafx-CD player that gives some games outstanding sound quality and also plays regular CDs

● The TurboPad controller with three-level turbo control

● The TurboStick with variable turbo fire and slow-motion features

● TurboTap adapter that lets as many five players play at the same time.

Genesis™
By: Sega

More memory than ever. That's what this new system promises. This 16-bit machine will feature better graphics, better sound, and much more complex game play than ever. New games are being created for it but it's also downward compatible, meaning that all Sega games out now can be played on it.

It's currently available in Japan but will be coming here soon, too.

Game Boy™
By: Nintendo

Game Boy is the Walkman™ of video game systems — the smallest one yet! It's also portable. Think of it as the Walkman of the video world. It has a tiny color screen, and the games come on pocket-size cards. Like the other new systems, it's out in Japan already and could be here very soon.

GAMES, GAMES, AND MORE GAMES

What would a video game system be without games? Not much! Watch for these new games that will soon be available for the Nintendo and Sega game systems.

For: Nintendo
By: Broderbund

The Battle of Olympus™

This game takes you to ancient Greece. You are Orpheus and you must save Helene, whose soul has been captured by the evil Hades. On your quest, you have to battle snakes, centaurs, a horrible hydra, and Cerberus the three-headed dog. If you like, you can customize the game so the characters call you by your name.

Deadly Towers™

Rubas, King of Devils, has built a castle in the northern part of the Kingdom of Willner. He is preparing to invade the kingdom by ringing magic bells and calling out an army of terrifying creatures. You, Prince Myer, must defeat him by journeying to his palace and burning down seven bell towers. Along the way you collect weapons and armor to defend yourself against rats, bats, snakes, slime demons, dragons, and other creatures too horrible to mention. And, once you get to the castle, there are over 1,500 rooms to explore.

The Guardian Legend™

Long ago in a distant galaxy, an alien race sent a huge planet called Naju hurtling toward Earth. It was loaded with a cargo of mysterious, evil life-forms. During the course of the long journey they increased in number and became even more evil. Deep within Naju are self-destruct devices that can destroy the planet before it reaches Earth — but only if they are activated. That's your job.

Legacy of the Wizard™

Many years ago, an evil dragon terrorized the forest. It was imprisoned by a powerful wizard. Now, the dragon has been released, and it's up to you to defeat him. To do this, you take on the identities of the members of the Draslef family, the Wizard's descendants. There's a father, a mother, a few kids, and even a pet. By switching from character to character, you can take advantage of their individual powers and strengths.

For: Sega

ALF™

Yes, ALF is coming right into your game room in this new game based on his life on Earth. You are ALF. You want to visit your friends, Skip and Rhonda on Mars, but you have a lot to do before you can get there. You have to fix your spaceship. Then you have to find a spacesuit, a giant pearl, a gold nugget, a costume, and a key. And don't forget to pick up a stick of salami. It will be good for knocking bats out of the air in underground caves.

Time Soldiers™

This is an adaptation of the popular arcade game. Five of your friends have been captured, turned into energy balls, and scattered through time. You have to find them and rescue them. A time scanner tells you where they are. But before you can set them free, you have to battle three sets of bosses, sub-bosses, and the evil galactic tyrant Gylend. They are some mean dudes! If you fail in your mission, Gylend will destroy Earth.

Rastan™

In this game, you're a barbarian who has to rescue the King's daughter from the clutches of the evil Lord of Semia. To do this, you have to travel to Semia, a place that's so horrible even the bad guys are scared. You start out with a sword. By feeding certain creatures, you can pick up a mace, a battle-ax, and a flaming sword. Other things you can use on your journey include a magic cloth that will wipe out all the enemies on the screen, armor, jewelry, and magic potions for strength. Be sure to avoid the poison. It won't help you at all.

Altered Beast™

This is the official home version of the number-one smash arcade hit of the same name. You're a Roman centurion brought back to life by Zeus, the King of the Gods. It seems Zeus wants you to rescue his daughter Athena from Neff, the evil Lord of the Underworld. On your journey, you must pick up three energy balls. The energy balls give you the power to turn into altered beasts: a Werewolf, a Weredragon, a Weretiger, and a golden Werewolf, the strongest of all. You'll need to become one or the other of these creatures to battle the ghouls, zombies, demons with giant hammers, and three-headed wolves you'll encounter in the Underworld. And, if that isn't enough, you'll then have to fight Neff himself!

Out Run 3-D™

This sequel to *Out Run* is made to be used with Sega's 3-D glasses. You're driving in a road rally, and you've got to make the best time ever.

Reggie Jackson Baseball™

Reggie Jackson himself helped put together this game. It's very interactive, and you can play with either the computer or a friend. At the end of the game, Reggie Jackson appears to compliment you on your game and to give you tips on how to improve your play.

Lord of the Sword™

You're a wandering lad with a sword in this adventure/

role-playing game. It's up to you to save the kingdom from the clutches of the evil Ragoan. You must perform three tasks set up by the King: find the tree of Merrill, the symbol of the royal family; defeat the evil goblin in Balala Valley; and destroy the evil statue. Along the way, you get involved in a number of side quests, including rescuing a princess, defeating five men in combat, and battling the swamp creature. Magic swords and bows and arrows that you find along the way will help you. Don't underestimate the power of the magic book. If you throw it in the Lake of Fire, it will destroy Ragoan's power.

Poseidon Wars 3-D ™

In this first game of the Poseidon series, you are a sailor. You attend the naval academy, graduate, and are put in command of the USS Poseidon. When your country is attacked, you help defend it by fighting enemy ships, planes, and submarines. If you defeat the enemy, you become an Admiral of the Fleet.

California Games ™

This is a series of games on one cartridge. You get to surf, play footbag, throw flying discs, ride a BMX, and do some fancy stunt skateboarding!

BONUS SEGA TIP: In *Phantasy Star,* you need a road pass. In the town of Scion, buy secrets *three times*. On the third time, you'll get a road pass.

CHAPTER SEVEN
The Player Connection

Save money! Meet new friends! See your name in print! How? By joining a video game club or forming one of your own.

GAME EXCHANGE-O-RAMA

Let's face it. After battling the Bacterion Empire one hundred times, you might get a little sick of *Gradius*. But Game Paks cost big bucks so you can't always afford to buy a new one. Don't worry. There are a couple of clubs where members buy and sell used games at very low prices. The following clubs are just a few of the many you can join. Before you join a club, decide whether the membership fee and what it brings you are worth it.

Play It Again

Play It Again is a video game club that buys and sells used Nintendo and Atari 2600 cartridges. As a member, you can sell your old Game Paks to the club and buy used cartridges at a discount price. A lifetime membership costs between $25 and $30. It will get you a 5% discount on all products, twelve price lists a year, and a free Play It Again T-shirt. Play It Again guarantees all their used Nintendo cartridges for one full year. For more information, send a note and a self-addressed, stamped envelope to:

Play It Again
Dept. BBC
P.O. Box 6718
Flushing, NY 11365

BONUS NINTENDO TIP: In *Double Dragon*, at the end of the second level, press "A," "B," and "Forward" together, and you'll get a super jump kick!

Video Replay

Here's another carts-for-cash club that buys and sells used Nintendo, Atari, and Sega cartridges. The best way to find out what they have to offer is to write to them and ask for their current price list. Send a note and a stamped, self-addressed envelope to:

Video Replay
P.O. Box 70
Jericho, NY 11753

Team Sega Game of the Month

Buy three, get one free! That's the Game of the Month

offer from Sega. Just fill out the card that comes with each game cartridge and mail it to Sega. After you've sent in three cards, Sega will send you one game free — the Sega Game of the Month.

Team Sega Newsletter
P.O Box 2167
573 Forbes Boulevard
South San Francisco, CA 94080

DO-IT-YOURSELF CLUBS

Starting your own club can be a great way to save money, make friends, and sharpen your game skills. The Videoizers in Massachusetts are a Nintendo video game club. They meet, play together, and trade cartridges and tips. They even pool their money to buy new games and to pay for calls to the Nintendo Hotline.

If this sounds like a fun-tastic idea to you, here are some pointers that will help you start your own club.

How to Start Your Own Club

1. Find kids who have the same game system as yours. Invite them to join the club.
2. Give yourselves a great name. Make it strong, snappy, and fun. Here are some suggestions. The VidKids. The Game Lords. The Nintendo Ninjas. The Segatrons. The Atari Masters. Now make up your own.
3. Decide what day each week you're going to meet. Decide where. It's probably a good idea to switch houses.
4. Hold contests. Choose one game at each meeting. Give each member a week to practice. Then have a play-off. See who can score the highest. See who discovers the most secrets. See who can get through the most levels without getting zapped.
5. Have a club treasury. Make money by doing odd jobs or by selling games that no one likes anymore or of which your club has extra copies. Use the money to buy new

games or accessories or to buy yourselves T-shirts with the name of your team on them.

6. Swap secrets and tips. Work together to find all the hidden treasures and get through all the levels of all games.

7. Write your own newsletter and send it to everyone who belongs to your club. Include game tips, high scores, and news about members. Give it a name. Here are some suggestions: *The Nintendo Ninja News* or *The Segatron Gazette* or *The Atari Masters Messenger*. Now make up your own.

BONUS NINTENDO TIP: In *Karate Kid*, jump into the black spaces to find bonus screens!

CHAPTER EIGHT
Questions and Answers

Here are answers to some of the most asked questions about the hot video games.

Q: Do video games hurt TV sets?

A: No. Not today's games, anyway. In the early days of video gaming it was a different story. The first ball-and-paddle games didn't always have built-in screens to protect the TV tubes. So the graphics sometimes left a permanent line running down the screen. Not anymore. You can play *Double Dragon* all you want. You'll never see Jimmy or Bill Lee show up in the middle of *ALF*!

Q: Can video games hurt your eyes?

A: So far, no one has been able to prove that they do.

Still, staring at any bright light for a long time can give you headaches and eyestrain. It's better to be safe than sorry. Follow these simple rules to keep your eyes in good shape:

1. Don't stare at the bright game screen for more than thirty minutes at a stretch. Give your eyes a rest.

2. Don't play video games in the dark.

3. Take regular breaks. Go outside to play catch. Draw. Do a somersault.

Q: Who invented the first home video game?

A: A lot of people think it was Nolan Bushnell. That's because *Pong* was the beginning of Atari's success. But before there was Atari, there was Odyssey™. In 1971, Ralph Baer and Magnavox, the company he worked for, came up with a programmable video game system and they called it Odyssey. One of the games Mr. Baer developed for Odyssey was a Ping-Pong simulation. It had a dotted line for a net and a pair of video paddles on either side of the playing field. The Odyssey system was nowhere when it came to background graphics. Instead, each game came with its own plastic overlay that players taped to their TV screens. If not for Mr. Baer, there might never have been Nintendo or Sega! Way to go, Mr. Baer!

Q: Is it true that Kirk Cameron likes to play Nintendo games?

A: It is true. Kirk is a real Nintendo fan. In between working on the show "Growing Pains" and traveling around telling kids about the dangers of drugs, Kirk likes to play his favorite games. He says he's rescued the princess in *Super Mario Brothers 2* "a million times." A lot of Kirk's friends play Nintendo, too. They all get together and share their game cartridges and know-how.

Q: Where are most video games designed?

A: During the first wave of video game mania, most games sold in the United States were designed here. Most games for today's sytems are designed in Japan, but quite a few come from France and England, too.

Q: How many hours a day do you have to practice to be really awesome?

A: Josh Reed has the answer. Josh is 13 years old and he's as close to being a professional Nintendo player as you can get. He plays Nintendo games in front of live audiences. Last summer Josh played Nintendo games at the Consumer Electronics Show in Las Vegas. "I used to practice 16 hours a day," says Josh. "I only came out of my room to eat breakfast and dinner." With so much practice, Josh became so good that he doesn't have to practice anymore. He can usually figure out brand-new games in less than one day. "In fact," says Josh, "it only took me four hours to win Trojan." Josh's highest scores are 9,999,999 on *Super Mario Brothers 2* and 675,000 on *Hogan's Alley.*®

Q: Are there any hotlines to call if you have a question or need help with a game?

A: Yes. Both Sega and Nintendo have hotlines. The Sega Hotline number is 1-800-USA-SEGA. The Nintendo Hotline number is 1-800-422-2602. Nintendo also has a Game Counselor Hotline you can call if you need to ask for help on a tough game. The number is 1-206-885-7529. This is a toll call, so ask your parents before you dial.

Q: What's it like to be a Nintendo game counselor?

A: Part of a game counselor's job is to play the games. Before you can become a game counselor, you go through a five-week training course, where you learn the secrets of the most popular games and how to answer questions from players. Once you're a counselor, you work eight-hour shifts, sometimes starting at four in the morning! And there's no time to sit around shooting the breeze with the other counselors either. You're too busy answering calls. More than 50,000 people call Nintendo for strategy tips each week. If there are 30 kids in your class, each of you would have to call the Hotline 1,666 times to make 50,000. Nintendo game counselors dress cool, too. They can buy their own Nintendo jackets with their names sewn right on the front.

Q: Do video games teach you anything?

A: They do. Video games can help sharpen your hand-eye coordination. What is hand-eye coordination? Think of it as the eye-brain-hand hookup. Your eye sees a blue bubble nearby in *Zelda II*. Your brain figures out what to do and tells your hands. Your hands then press the direction controller, move your character over to the bubble, and, bingo, you have your sword back! Another example of hand-eye coordination is the skill of catching a baseball.

Video games also help you learn, concentrate, and remember. A quick look at *Castlevania* will prove this point. After jumping too early and getting bonked on the head by a flying Medusa, you learn to jump later. If you have a hard time getting past the crushing machine without getting crushed, you concentrate on figuring out when the crushers are up so you can dash through safely. If you whip a stone wall and find a crown, you'll remember that crown again the next time you play.

It's not a good idea to sit inside and play video games all day long. Be careful — you don't want to get addicted! Go outside and have fun. The beauty of these games is that they'll always be there to pick up where you've left off. The fresh air will clear your brain and help you beat Big Boss Wart next time.

Q: Are Mario and Luigi going to have their own TV show?

A: Yes. The jumping Mario Brothers are going to star in their own live-action cartoon show starting in September 1989. Watch the TV schedule in your area so you don't miss it. And while you're at it, you'd better watch your supermarket shelves, too. The Brothers are going to have their own breakfast cereal, too. Mario and Luigi will be lemon-flavored, and other Nintendo game characters will taste like berries.

~~~~~~

BONUS NINTENDO TIP: In *Double Dragon*, on level 3, go into the caves of the Abobos. If you don't, you'll keep going around and around and around!

~~~~~~